PRAYER

FOR

SINGLES

08023583168

TELLA OLAYERI

All rights reserved under International Copyright Law. Content may not be reproduced in whole or in part or in any form without the consent of the publisher.

Email; tellaolayeri@gmail.com
Website tellaolayeri.com.ng

US Contact
Ruth Jack
14 Milewood Road
Verbank
N.Y.12585
U.S.A. +19176428989

APPRECIATION

I give special appreciation to my wife **MRS NGOZI OLAYERI** for her assistance in ensuring that this book is published and our children that play around us to encourage us day and night.

Also, this manuscript wouldn't have seen the light of the day, if not for the spiritual encouragement I gathered from my father in the Lord, **Dr. D.K. OLUKOYA** who served as spiritual mirror that brightens my hope to explore my calling (Evangelism).

We shall all reap our blessings in heaven but the battle to make heaven is not over, until it is won.

PREVIOUS PUBLICATIONS OF THE AUTHOR

1. Fire for Fire Prayer Book Part 1

2. Fire for Fire Prayer Book Part 2

3. Bye Bye to Poverty Part 1

4. Bye Bye to Poverty Part 2

5. My Marriage Shall Not Break

6. Prayer for Pregnant Women

7. Prayer for Fruit of the Womb

8. Children Deliverance

9. Prayer for Youths and Teenagers

10. Magnetic Prayer for Singles

11. Victory over satanic house Part 1

12. Victory over satanic house Part 2

13. I Shall Excel

14. Atomic Prayer Points

15. Goliath at the gate of marriage

16. Deliverance from Spirit of Dogs

17. Naked warriors

18. Power to Overcome Sex in the Dream

19. Strange Women! Leave My Husband Alone

PRAYER FOR SINGLES

20. *Dangerous Prayer against Strange Women*

21. *Solution to Unemployment*

22. *630 Acidic Prayer Points*

23. *Prayer for Job Seekers*

24. *Power to Retain Job and Excel in Office*

25. *Warfare in the Office*

26. *Power to Overcome Unprofitable Wealth*

27. *Command the Year*

28. *Deliverance Prayer for First Born*

29. *Deliverance Prayer for Good Health and Divine Healing*

30. *Warfare Prayer against Untimely Death.*

31. *Dictionary of Dreams*

32. *Discover Gold and Build Wealth*

33. *My Head is not for Sale*

34. *830 Prophecies for the head*

35. *30 Power Points for the Head*

36. *Prayer after Dreams*

37. *Prayer to Locate Helpers*

38. *Anointing for Eleventh Hour Help*

39. *100% Confessions and Prophecies to Locate Helpers*

40. *Hidden Treasures Exposed!*

41. *Prayer to Cancel Bad Dreams*

42. *Prayer to Remember Dreams*

43. *1010 Dreams and interpretations*

44. *650 Dreams and Interpretation*

45. *1,000 Prayer Points for Children Breakthrough*

46. *Emergency telephone calls of God*

47. *I Am Not Alone*

48. *My Well of Honey shall not dry*

49. *Shake Heaven with Praises*

50. *Deliverance prayer for Middle Born Part One*

51. *800 Deliverance prayer for Middle Born Part Two*

52. *Deliverance prayer for Last Born Part One*

53. *800 Deliverance prayer for Last Born Part Two*

PRAYER FOR SINGLES

Table of Contents

OPENING PRAYER 8
POWER TO WAGE SPIRITUAL WARFARE 19
VIOLENT PRAYER AND BATTLE 24
BREAKING THE YOKE OF MARRITAL FAILURE 30
OPERATION BREAK WICKED WORKS. 35
REVOKING WICKED DECREE 38
PRAYER THAT REVERSES EVIL PRONOUNCEMENT 42
WARFARE AGAINST MARRIAGE CRUSHERS 49
WARFARE AGAINST SPIRIT SPOUSE 52
PRAYER FOR RIGHT SPOUSE 56
PRAYER FOR MALE ONLY 57
PRAYER FOR FEMALES ONLY 59
WEDDING DAY PRAYER 61
MY FAVOUR AND MERCY IS TODAY 66
STRONG POSITIVE CONFESSIONS 68

CHAPTER ONE

OPENING PRAYER
THANKSGIVING

I thank you O Lord for making things work together for good in my life. I pay for foods I eat, pay for light bills, rents etc, but not for my existence on earth, or for sight, walk or for speech. If I should pay for these bills I will go bankrupt. Your word says **"... *young lion do lack, and suffer hunger but they that seek the LORD shall not want any good thing". Psalm 34: 1** Instead of going bankrupt, my plan now is to wed. To this I give you total glory and adoration.

O Lord you are mighty and bigger than very problem, as none can swallow or suppress you. You have power to cheat but you never did. You have power to do evil but you never do. You are the King of kings and the Lord of lords, the unchangeable changer, I AM that I AM; the Alpha and Omega.

I thank you Lord as you shall finance and uphold my marriage. I thank you Lord that you shall take over my burden. I thank you Lord of the anointing of happiness, joy, promotion, wealth, prosperity and good health upon my life. I thank you Lord that my marriage shall come to pass very soon.

I thank you Lord for the salvation of my soul and for empowering me through in prayer. I thank you Lord for intervening in my situation and for forth coming marriage that shall be of glory unto you. For it is written, *'Therefore, the redeemed of the LORD shall return, and come with singing unto Zion and everlasting joy shall be upon their head: they shall obtain gladness and joy, and sorrow and mourning shall flee away"* Isaiah 51:11.

(NOW SING THIS SONG WITH JOY IN YOUR HEART)
I WILL SING UNTO THE LORD
A JOYFUL SONG
I WILL PRAISE HIS NAME
FOR THE LORD IS GOOD
HALLELUJAH

"With my whole being I sing for joy to the living God" Psalm 84:2B. *"I will praise God's name in song and glorify him with thanksgiving" Psalm 69:30.* I thank you Lord for praises that proceeds from my mouth. I thank you Lord for protecting me from the snares of the fowler and noisome pestilence.

FORGIVENESS OF SIN

O Lord, I come before you as a sinner for the forgiveness of my sin, as it is written *"He who conceals his sins does not prosper, but whoever confessed and renounces them finds mercy"*

Proverbs 28:13. Have mercy upon me O Lord my God; *"wash away all my iniquity and cleanse me from my sin" Psalm 51:2*. O Lord I pray for forgiveness of my sin because it rests with you. Envelop me with spirit of humility that breaks uncircumcised heart. Let every seed of hell in me roast to ashes in the name of Jesus.

Use your rod and your staff to comfort me. Prepare a table of victory before me in the presence of my enemies, anoint my head with oil of goodness. Wipe tears in my face and a stop to my weep. Do not set your face against me but favour me; *"when we were overwhelmed by sins, you forgave our transgression" Psalm 65:3*. O Lord forgive me, for *"you do not stay angry forever but delight to show mercy" Micah 7:18.*

O Lord, forgive me the sins of my father's house and of my mother's house that may work against me. In your infinite mercy Lord, answer me, for your anger lasts only for a moment while your favour lasts a lifetime. Let my prayer ascend to heaven. Turn my wailing to dancing, remove my sackcloth and clothe me with garment of joy so that my heart may sing unto you.

NOW SING THIS SONG WITH ALL SERIOUSNESS
**WHO IS LIKE UNTO THEE O LORD
WHO IS LIKE THEE**

AMONG THE gods WHO IS LIKE THEE
GLORIOUS IN HOLINESS
FEARFUL IN PRAISES
DOING WONDERS HALLELUJAH.

O Lord, quench the lamp of the wicked against my life because the lamp of the wicked is sin! My Lord and my God, wash my stain garment so that l may be accepted before you. Have compassion upon me and tread my sin under your feet.

(BE ON YOUR KNEE AS YOU PRAY THESE PARAGRAPHS IN SOBER MOOD AND SUPPLICATION)

O Lord my God, I am ashamed and full of disgrace to lift up my eyes before you because my sins are higher than my head and my guilt has reached heavens. In fact I am a disgrace before you. *"To you I call, O LORD my ROCK, do not turn a deaf ear to me. For if you remain silent, I will be like those who have gone down to the pit. Hear my cry for mercy as I call to you for help, as I lift up my hands towards your most High Place" Psalm28:1-2* O Lord my redeemer show me mercy and kindness. I know I have not acted well by not obeying your commandments, rules and decrees; pardon me Lord put them out of sight, out of reach, out of mind and out of existence.
"I was ashamed and humiliated because I love the disgrace of my youth" Jeremiah 31:19b. For I

mingled with ungodliness, deep hands into impurity, enter where I shouldn't, slept on beds I shouldn't and ate foods I shouldn't. I lost my virginity before marriage. All these now stand against me. My accuser, Satan is strongly opposed to me. Now, there is no one I can call for help except you. Therefore Lord, help me and forgive me. Lord Jesus, I realize my sins, **"For God hath not called us unto uncleanness but unto holiness" Thess.4:7.** O Lord, **"Remember yet not the former things; neither consider the things of old" Isaiah 43:18.**

From youth till date, my guilt has been much. My sins have naked me before my enemies and rendered me powerless before my detractors. It gives enemies opportunity to attack me from all directions. O Lord, do not be hostile to my pleas, save me and forgive me.

My cup has overflowed with sins. My bed turned to palace of thinking in respect of lust. My Lord and my God, **"Remember not the sins of my youth and my rebellious ways, according to your love remember me for you are good O Lord" Psalm 25:7.** Holy Spirit break me down for **"without holiness no one will see the Lord" Hebrew 12:14.** I plead O Lord I shall not go back into sin anymore.
(NOW STAND UP AND CONTINUE WITH YOUR PRAYER)

BLOOD OF JESUS

O Lord, cleanse me with your blood save me from self acclaim righteousness. For, *"there is not a righteous man on earth who does what is right and never sins"*
Ecclesiastes 7:20. Blood of Jesus, flow within me, flow around me, flow upon me. By the power in the blood of Jesus, I command sins and ungodliness, idolatry and vices in me to cease by fire. By this, I wash my hands with blood of Jesus from filths (do as if you are washing your hands) and declare as follows: Mention your name and declare like this:- *"Have nothing to do with worthless things that people do, things that belong to the darkness" Ephesians 5:11*.

NOW SING THIS SONG AND CONTINUE WITH YOUR PRAYER.
THE BLOOD OF JESUS
THE BLOOD OF JESUS SET ME FREE
FROM SIN AND SORROW
THE BLOOD OF JESUS SET ME FREE
I plead the blood of Jesus upon my life, upon my destiny, upon my calling and upon my career. Hence Lord, cleanse me of blood pollution that placed me under spiritual and physical arrest. Save and cleanse me Oh Lord for *"No soap can wash away my sins" Job 9:30,* except with your unpolluted blood. Hence, 1 soak my name, my destiny, my future and career in the pull blood of

Jesus. Lord Jesus fertilize every seed of faithfulness in me so that I might walk blameless before you. For, *"to the faithful you show yourself faithful, to the blameless you show yourself blameless" Psalm 18:25.*

O Lord let your blood be a source of healing to my spirit, soul and body. Let your healing power begin in my life right now. I wash and cleanse my garment and that of my spouse in the pool blood of Jesus, as it is written, **"They have washed their robes and made them white in the blood of the lamb" Revelation 7:14B.** I purge my foundation; purge my life and destiny of evil deposits with blood of Jesus. Every spirit that entered me through curse or evil covenant shall be purged by blood of Jesus. I drink blood of Jesus *(with faith say this seven times and do as if you are drinking it)*. I drink blood of Jesus, to dissolve and destroy evil deposits in me, evil plantation growing secretly in my body and every affliction troubling my life. O Lord, purge me of evil thoughts, circumcise me with your power and blood. By the power in your blood, break and dissolve covenant of failure and evil dedication made on my behalf. Blood of Jesus flow in my life, anointing of God push me to marital breakthrough, in the name of Jesus. As I purge myself, let the story of my *life* change in the name of Jesus.

Inject me with your blood; show yourself mightily in my life. Heal and brighten my hope, *for hope deferred makes the heart sick" Proverbs 13:12.* Strengthen my faith for *"faith is being sure of what we hope for" Hebrew 11:1.* Let your blood in my life be a sign of protection against wicked powers in the order of Israelites on the eve of Passover. By this, let late marriage, poverty, loneliness, borrowing, stagnancy, ill-luck etc pass over me, for it is written *"And when I see the blood I will pass over you" Exodus 12:13.*

Blood of Jesus set me free from spiritual imprisonment that makes marital expectation difficult. Blood of Jesus paralyze and destroy demons troubling me in my father's and in my mother's house. Blood of Jesus silence every rage of witchcraft against me and swallow negative power battling with my peace. Blood of Jesus nullify anger of the enemy against my life.

Blood of Jesus cleanse me, warm what is cold in me, bend what is stiff in me and heal every wound in me. The Bible says, *"Though your sins be as scarlet, they shall be as white as snow, though they be red like crimson, they shall be as white as wool". Isaiah 1:18.* Therefore Satan stop accusing me for I am cleansed with blood of Jesus. *"The Lord rebuke you" Jude 1:9,* therefore shut up! I thank you Lord that I am protected by the wonder working power in your word and by the blood of the lamb. Amen.

HOLY SPIRIT AND FIRE

Fresh fire from heaven, fall upon me. Holy Spirit, incubate me with power that shall make me a conqueror. Holy Ghost Power, flood me with light of deliverance in the order of Paul on his way to Damascus. *"Create in me a clean heart, O God, and renew a right spirit within me" Psalm 51:10*. Holy Spirit, fill me with spirit of revival. Prince of peace change my destiny, reign in every department of my life.

Holy Ghost Fire, keep my lamps burning turn darkness in my life to light. O Lord, let your fire generate power in my life. Holy Spirit, seize power that enemies rely upon to destroy me. Baptize me with overdose power that shall turn my life around.

Holy Spirit divine bind and disgrace every strongman in charge of my situation. O Lord, let your angels be in charge of my affairs. Holy Ghost Fire set ablaze and roast to ashes wrong foundation and wicked mountains troubling my destiny. Holy Spirit Divine rain stones of fire upon satanic operations troubling my life.

Holy Ghost Fire, burn to ashes evil altars in the corridor of my life. Fire of God destroy effects of idolatry, sacrifice, rituals, shrines etc working against me. Holy Ghost Power, dethrone and disgrace powers of strange parent, strange brothers, strange sisters and strange relatives causing confusion in my life. Satan you shall fail because *"... my Lord is with me like a mighty warrior; so my persecutors will stumble and not prevail" Jeremiah 20:11.*

Holy Spirit be my partner in this battle *"For we wrestle not against flesh and blood, but against principalities, against powers, against spiritual wickedness in high places" Ephesians 6:12.* I encircle and electrify myself and environment with fire of Holy Ghost. Fresh anointing of God that disgrace problems fall upon me. Anointing that break the yoke fall upon me. Anointing that cannot be insulted fall upon me. My spirit refuse to wonder around as I pray, my hands cooperate with me, my mouth cooperate with me, my legs cooperate with me, in the name of Jesus, amen.

Holy Spirit, by your power circumcise my heart, fill my mouth with your word, remold me for your purpose. Cleanse my heart of evil thoughts and plans that may ruin my life, my calling and marriage, in the name of Jesus. Holy Spirit, heal the wound in my heart and pour anointing of gladness upon me. O Lord, remove spirit of flesh in me, awake my spirit, soul and body. Holy Ghost Fire, deliver me and flush my system of contamination for it is written, *"upon mount Zion shall be deliverance, and there shall be holiness, and the house of Jacob shall possess their possessions" Obadiah 1:17.*

NOW SING THIS SONG THREE TIMES.
SEND DOWN FIRE
THE HOLY GHOST FIRE
SEND DOWN FIRE AGAIN
THE HOLY GHOST FIRE

Holy Ghost Fire move into action now and locate my future partner for me. For it is written, *"Two are better than one, because they have a good return for their work" Ecclesiastes 4:9.* In my marriage, establish sit of victory for me. For it is written, *"The LORD himself goes before you and will be with you, he will never leave you nor forsake you. Do not be afraid, do not be discouraged" Deuteronomy 31:8.*

CHAPTER TWO

POWER TO WAGE SPIRITUAL WARFARE

My God that hear what ordinary ear cannot hear, my God that sees what ordinary eyes cannot see, be my deliverer. Thou heaven open, let my voice and prayer ascend to heaven. Whatever I say come to pass, whatever I command stand firm. Brave warriors of heaven, commanders of host of heaven, gather together now. Arm yourselves for this battle; roll out tanks and warfare armaments fight this battle for me. Purge when you should purge, paralyse when you should paralyse, bind when you should bind, kill when you should kill, destroy when you should destroy, hang wicked powers when occasion demands for it and bury when you should bury. Foil the plans of the enemy against me and thwart their efforts against my life, in the name of Jesus. Amen.

In this battle train my hands to war and my fingers to battle. (*Now, raise up your hand, shake it and say this three times*). My hand shall not trade with failure, shall not trade with failure, shall not trade with failure! in the name of Jesus. Amen. My hands shall bring victory in the name of Jesus. (*Now relax your hands and pray on*).

O Lord my God, stretch your hand of deliverance upon me. Hosts of heaven dress me and equip me with arrow- proofed and bullet-proofed jackets against warfare arrows and bullets. Umbrella of God protect me in this battle, save me from wicked arrows of the enemy. Hence, I command every wicked arrow of fornication, of anger, pride, poverty, sorrow and tragedy fired against me to backfire by fire.

(NOW TOUCH YOUR CHEST AND SAY)

My heart and soul, receive divine healing, receive divine *support,* receive divine fire, for *"The LORD is close to the broken hearted and saves those who are crushed in spirit" Psalm 34:18.* My spirit man, fear not this battle is yours. Trumpet of joy locate my mouth as I shall triumph over my enemies. My spouse, wherever you are, locate me by fire. *"My dove in the clefts of the rock, show me your face, let me hear your voice, for your voice is sweet, and your face is lovely" Songs of Solomon* 2:14. As wisdom is better than folly and light better than darkness so is marriage better than darkness and loneliness. O Lord, perfect my life, give me right spouse that shall strengthen and elevate me. Wherever my spouse is, arrest and direct him/her to me. If he/she is in the world right now touch his/her heart for good. Bless him/her to see importance in marriage.

O Lord I am mature in all forms to marry, yet I am single and unmarried. At present, I am ... years old

(mention your age), come to my situation now and help
me out, for the Holy Bible says *"There is time for everything, and a season for everything and a season or every activity under heaven:*
A time to be born and a time .to die,
A time to plant and a time to uproot,
A time to kill and a time so heal,
A time to tear down and a time to build,
A time to weep and a time to laugh.

Therefore Lord let this hour be my time of laughter. O Lord, this is not the time or hour I should be single; let me experience marital breakthrough. Change my state of singleness to marriage hood. Restore my lost hopes. Fulfill your promise, change my trial to testimony and envelop me with dumbfounding marital breakthroughs. Let secret tears disappear in my face. Let this season be my season, let this month be my month, let this week be my week, let this day be my day, let this hour be my hour, in the name of Jesus. Amen. Let answer and solution to my prayer appear now. Deliver me oh Lord for my time is now not tomorrow. Speak to my situation now oh Lord my God, people are asking me, *"why does your face look so sad when you are not ill? This can he nothing hut sadness of heart"* Nehemiah 2:2. In this battle Lord, let my enemies experience defeat and failure. Pull down evil altars trading with my destiny. Smash sacred stones pulling me down.

Cut down evil poles and pillars hindering my marriage. Fight this battle for me so that my name shall not disappear in my lineage.

Holy Ghost Power, bind and paralyze enemies of my soul. For it is written, *"Can anyone enter .a strongman's house except he is first bound" Mathew* 12: 29. Therefore bind territorial powers supervising my life. Thou strongman of my father's house and of my mother's house, boasting against my marriage I bind you by fire. For it is written *in Mathew 16*:19 "I will give you the keys of the kingdom of heaven whatever you bind on earth will be bound in heaven and whatever you loose on earth will be loosed in heaven" Therefore, I bind powers and principalities holding my life to ransom.

Holy Michael, Arch angel of God lead, other host of angels like swarms of locust to scatter and bombard the camp of the enemy. Frighten them out of my home. Thou enemies of my soul, whatever you gather to harm me shall scatter, the weapons you rely upon shall fail, every tact you know shall disgrace you, in the name of Jesus. Thou powers from the desert, from the ocean, from the .second heaven or beneath the earth delegated against me die, in the name of Jesus. Rock of .Ages; grind into powder every instrument of darkness gathered for my sake. Afflict my enemies with blindness and madness. Empty their powers and render them powerless. Hence, I alight from wrong vehicle and take right vehicle of perfection, in the name of Jesus.

O Lord, provide me with what I shall need to see me through in life. My Lord and my God arise, deliver me from satanic Herod delegated against me. Deliver me from hands of family Herod, hands of office Herod and hands of dream Herod in the name of Jesus. Amen. Let every anti progress material in me suffocate in the blood of Jesus. Let every power energizing and compounding problems in me come out by fire and die. Let every power assign to swallow my testimony vomit them now and die. Let witchcraft darkness in my life disappear by fire in the name of Jesus.

CHAPTER THREE

VIOLENT PRAYER AND BATTLE

Anything around me, anything within me, hear the word of the Lord, you must cooperate with me by fire. Host of heaven declare war; declare unprecedented bombardment of artilleries and armaments against powers fashioned against me. Empower me Lord to subdue and destroy every power roaring like lion against my life. For it is written, "I pursue my enemies and overtook them, I did not turn back till they were destroyed. 1 crush them so that they could not rise, they fell beneath my feet" Psalm 18:37-38. The battle is today and now, therefore I command every Iron Gate holding me captive to open by fire. O Lord as I pray let my voice cause confusion, cause delay, cause destruction and death in the camp of enemies. As this battle proceeds, let it get hot against contrary powers within and around me. The wicked shall fail concerning my situation. For, "the wicked roar and growl like lions but God silences them and breaks their teeth" Job 4:10. At midday my enemies shall grope about like blind men in the dark, while at night they shall fail at every step take. Every power planning to intercept my miracle this year, die. Thou principalities and powers that want this week bitter for me, that want this month bitter for me, that want this year bitter for me, shall die in the name of Jesus.

My Father, fight this battle for me. "Contend, O Lord with those who contend with me, fight against those who fight against me, from achieving my marital breakthrough. Psalm 35:1. By fire by force break the stubborn pride of my enemies. Let my enemies flee and run race of madness even when no one pursue them. Let my enemies reverse their steps and flee before me as one fleeing from the sword.

Enough is enough, before I go into marriage I shall not lose my spouse, on my wedding day, I shall not lose my spouse, after my wedding I shall not lose my spouse, in the name of Jesus. Amen. I pray against marital problems in my lineage, all going and coming back problems in my life. I shall not experience defeat in my marital pursuit, in the name of Jesus. Hence, I command every power that wants to shipwreck my marriage that wants to push me aside, or pull me down to die by the sword of God.

Angels of the living God don't compromise with enemies. In your anger Lord, be hostile to my enemies. Fire of God pursue my stubborn pursuers to the grave. Let disgrace, defeat and destruction be the portion of wicked powers delegated against me. Quench their wicked light against me, destroy their instrument of destruction . *Brandish spear and javelin against those who pursue me. Say to my soul, "I am your salvation" Psalm 35:3.* Thou enemies of my soul, my God shall confuse and shatter your confidence. *"As you do not know the path of the wind or how the body is formed in a mother's womb, so you cannot understand the work of God, the Maker of all things" Eccls.11: 5.* Therefore your efforts to frustrate me from marrying shall fail, in the name of Jesus. Satanic hunters of my joy receive double frustration. Any power that wants to naked me, go naked and die in the name of Jesus. Every masquerade pursuing me to cause marital failure and delay in my life die in the name of Jesus.

Holy Ghost Power, pursue every pursuer and destroy every destroyer assign against me. Fire your devouring arrow against stubborn pursuers and lay upon them heaps of calamities. Fire arrow of destruction into their camps, throw them into confusion and disarray with no one to rescue or pity them. Every satanic' ambush laid in readiness to destabilize my marital life scatter by fire.
NOW SING THIS WARFARE SONG THREE TIMES AND PRAY ON
HOLY GHOST PURSUE PURSUERS
DESTROY DESTROYERS
PURSUE PURSUERS
DESTROY DESTROYERS
HOLY GHOST FIRE, HOLY GHOST FIRE
HOLY GHOST FIRE, HOLY GHOST FIRE.

PRAYER FOR SINGLES

As fish are caught in a cruel net, or birds taken in a snare, so shall enemies of my soul be caught unaware. O Lord punish the acts of my enemies for attacking me seven times and over. Make the sky above them like *iron* and the ground beneath them like bronze. Every flying power delegated against my life fall down and die. Thou wicked power delegated against me you are under arrest, therefore face Holy Ghost firing square and die. For it is written, *"therefore shall evil come upon thee, thou shalt not know from whence it riseth: mischief shall fall upon thee, thou shalt not be to put it off: and desolation shall come upon thee suddenly which thou shalt not know"* Isaiah 47:11.

O Lord, destroy every high place of my enemies, cut down their *incense* and altars. Every contrary structure mounted against heavenly program for my life be dismantled by fire. Every idol of my family's house troubling me for evil be silence forever. Thou power causing unfruitfulness in my life, what are you waiting for, run mad and die. Thou pursuers of my soul as you flee fall by the sword.

NOW SING THIS SONG AS YOU PRAY ON
WHO CAN BATIL KWITH THE LORD?
WHO CAN BATTLE WITH THE LORD?
WHO CAN BATTLE WITH THE LORD?
I SAY NOBODY I SAY NOBODY.
I SAY NOBODY I SAY NOBODY.

My enemies fall into deep sleep and rise no more *in* the name of Jesus. Any power planning to waste me, be wasted. O Lord, sweep the wicked with broom of destruction and destroy evil plantation drawing me backward from reaching my mountain of success.

Holy Ghost Power, strike down every enemy of my soul with your power and encircle them with fire of sorrow. Wasting diseases and terror catch *up* with wicked powers delegated against me. Power of calamity, overtake my enemies like storm, strong disaster sweep them off like whirlwind, baptize them with fire of destruction in the name of Jesus. O Lord destroy their rod of fury, make them reap their wickedness, multiply their afflictions, weaken their strength. *"Arise, O Lord! Deliver me, o my God! Strike all my enemies on the jaw; break the teeth of the wicked"* Psalm 3:7. Let loud and bitter cry be their portion with no one to appease them.

Sword of destruction, locate and destroy any power pursuing me. Thou rebellious and troubleshooting agenda fashioned against my marriage catch fire, in the name of Jesus. Wicked powers delegated against me I pull down your altar and command acidic fire to consume you. Thou wicked and terrible power of my father's house and of my mother's house in charge of my life, lose your hold and die. Thou ancient gate of problems tormenting my life your time is *up*, therefore break, catch fire and roast to ashes. Thou serpent of darkness delegated against me be electrocuted by fire of God.

Any power holding night vigil against me, run mad and die. Internal enemy of my soul die, external enemy of my soul be crushed to pieces in the name of Jesus. Every wicked power tying down the horse of my marriage to a *spot,* die. Every power drawing energy from the sun, drawing energy from the moon, drawing energy from the star, drawing energy from the cloud, drawing energy from the sea, drawing energy from the rock, drawing energy from evil trees and evil altars, in order to destroy me die, in the name of Jesus. My star, my destiny, my marriage, *"arise, shine, for thy light is come and the glory of the LORD is risen upon thee"* Amen. *Isaiah 60:1.*

CHAPTER FOUR

BREAKING THE YOKE OF MARRITAL FAILURE

Holy Ghost Power incubate me with fire that shall destroy enemy of my soul, enemy of my marriage and enemy of my destiny. Since, *"the hand of the Lord is not too short to save, nor his ear too dull to hear" Isaiah* 59:1, *my* cry shall ascend to heaven for quick and immediate answer. Hence, I command every .satanic authority and dominion over me to break. Holy Ghost Power, locate and pull my spouse out of danger. My *spouse,* I say come out and locate me by fire. I command your spirit to come out of the grave, come out of the valley, come out of wilderness, come out of loneliness, come out of dryness, come out of poverty, and sorrow, *in* the name of Jesus. My spouse, receive freedom and deliverance from the hands of the wicked. I say receive liberation from powers of emptiness.

This year my marriage shall come to pass in the name of Jesus. My partner shall locate me and not be a thorn in my flesh in the name of Jesus. By this, we shall live at peace, for it is written *"If two lie down together, they will keep warm. But how can one keep warm alone? Ecclesiastes* 4:11.

Hence, my marriage shall not experience frustration in the name of Jesus. Amen.

Evil magnet drawing me from marital success, scatter. Every claim Satan relied against me shall fail. Every consequence of parental mistake troubling my life be nullified. Every circle of vanity surrounding my situation be nullified, in the name of Jesus. Stronghold of stagnancy and failure fashioned against my marriage break. Any power trying to frustrate God's plan for me, meet double failure. Thou cloud of darkness surrounding my destiny for failure disappear by fire. Every Red sea separating me from my marriage dry up by fire. My life is not for failure therefore any spirit of failure in me shall die in the name of Jesus.

Every problem that trouble my lineage and is now troubling me shall die. O Lord, heal my foundation, for **"If the foundation be destroyed, what the righteous can do" Psalm 11:3.** Every serpentine covenant in my foundation break, foundational curses troubling my life break, foundational covenant holding me captive break, foundational bondage holding me to square one break, foundational problem causing me sorrow and backwardness break in the name of Jesus. Hence Lord, build my marriage on strong and unpolluted foundation.

Every covenant of death upon my life and that of my spouse break in the name of Jesus. Covenant of untimely death and delay operating in my marriage break in the name of Jesus. Thou poison of darkness in my life melt away in the name of Jesus. Thou inherited pollution in me come out as vapour and disappear. Thou mark of death awaiting maturity in my life die, in the name of Jesus.

Any power searching for my face in evil mirror, go blind and run mad in the name of Jesus. Household wickedness against my life die, in the name of Jesus. Serpent of darkness fashioned against me die. Thou enemies of my soul, your plan to rob me shall not hold but fail. Wicked counselors hired to discourage me, hired to work against me or frustrate my plan, meet double failure in the name of Jesus. Wicked investigator assign to monitor my life go blind and die. For it is written in *Isaiah 41:11. "All who rage against you (that is me) will surely be ashamed and be disgraced; those who oppose you will be as nothing and perish"*.

Every garment of shame, of marital failure and sorrow, design by household wickedness against my life roast to ashes in the name of Jesus. O Lord, remove garment of shame in me and replace it with garment of acceptance, favour, success and breakthrough in the name of Jesus. Every poison of marital failure in my destiny be neutralized and be ineffective. Every influence of witchcraft in my life break. Every chain of hardship and poverty in my life, break. Demonic chain holding me to square one break. Stubborn cord holding me to marital failure break. By this, I break and lose myself from every form of inherited bondage, collective bondage and personal bondage in the name of Jesus. Amen.

Lord Jesus by the blood you shed on the cross of Calvary cleanse me of mark of failure, mark of hatred, mark of stagnancy, mark of backwardness, mark of trouble, mark of indebtedness and mark of loneliness. Cleanse me of satanic mark operating on my forehead. Blood of Jesus cleanse every spot and mark chasing opposite sex from me. My spirit, soul and body, shall not be ruined by powers of darkness.

Every evil mark placed on me from the day I was born till this day, I wipe you off by the blood of Jesus. Every evil mark I acquire from my mother's womb be cleansed by the blood of Jesus. Every evil mark waiting for maturity date in my life die now, in the name of Jesus. Every mark of backwardness, mark of delay, mark of stagnancy, mark of sorrow, mark of tragedy, mark of failure upon my life disappear by fire, in the name of Jesus.
I convert and reverse evil mark on me. Hence Lord, convert every mark of death placed upon me

to mark of life. Convert every mark of hatred in me to mark of love and every mark of failure in me to mark of success, in the name of Jesus.

CHAPTER FIVE

OPERATION BREAK WICKED WORKS.

I lift my hands in triumph to subdue and destroy works of darkness, as it is written, *"Your hand will be lifted up in triumph over your enemies, all your foes will be destroyed" Micah* **5:9**. Hence, I empower my hand with fire of Holy Ghost and exercise judgment against every curse, every contrary decree and commandments working against me. I cancel every agreement with marital demotion. I break and destroy conjuring mirror fashioned against me. I break and destroy every yoke against my marriage. I break and destroy every curse placed upon my marriage.

O Lord release more fire and energy on me to fight this battle. Let me tread upon serpents and scorpions unhurt. Bring Satan and his agents down on their knees, for you said, *"Behold I give unto you power to tread on serpents and scorpions, and over all the power of the enemy and nothing shall by any means hurt you" Luke* **10:19**.

Hence, I break and scatter evil gang up against me. I break and destroy jaw of poverty in my life. I break and destroy wicked powers and authorities assign against me. I break and destroy powers of persistent oppression and exploitation against me. I break and destroy presence of demonic influence upon my finance and destiny. I break and destroy evil altars firing arrows against my life, for it is written. *"Every plant, which my heavenly father hath not planted, shall be rooted up" Matthew 15:13.*

I redeem myself from conscious and unconscious slavery, and every affliction of the wicked. You heaven break every instrument of affliction fashioned against me. It is a rule that slaves do not go into marriage, I am neither a slave nor a slave's child, I am a child of Abraham, Father of faith. Therefore, anyone or power that labeled me "unmarriable" shall fail. Hence, I break every curse of slavery passed against me. I nullify negative pronouncement of thou shall remain single passed against me. I break power of polygamy that may affect my marriage. I break and cancel consequence of immoralities with people. I break every curse received due to promise and fail with opposite sex.

I command every witchcraft Pharaoh assign to disgrace me or hold me against my wish and conscience to release me and die. I apply hammer of God against problems facing me. I break every yoke of loneliness and marital failure troubling my life. Any power waiting to rejoice over my down fall shall fail. Every knee of darkness assign against me shall break. Every evil pot cooking my glory shall break to pieces, in the name of Jesus.

Thou padlock of darkness used to lock my marriage break. Personal chain in my life break, ancestral chain in my life break, lineage chain of sorrow in my life break, chain of stagnancy in my life break in the name of Jesus.

CHAPTER SIX

REVOKING WICKED DECREE

My foundation, receive deliverance from every form of darkness. Thou enemies of my soul, no matter how fast you run my God shall overtake, arrest and destroy you in the name of Jesus. Every certificate of failure operating in my family line, operating in my office, operating in my house and business catch fire and roast to ashes. Riches of this earth locate me now, for the Lord said in *Isaiah 61:6b, "You will feed on the wealth of nations, and in their riches you will boast".*

Therefore, every power marking evil calendar to destroy my joy shall meet double failure, in the name of Jesus. Every decree of loneliness pronounced against my life be revoked. Every verdict of failure operating within me, operating around me, operating upon me, be cancelled in the name of Jesus.

O carpenters of heaven dismantle and destroy every instrument of wickedness and evil roadblock mounted against my marital vehicle. *"Plead my cause O LORD, with them that strive with me: fight against them that fight against me. Take hold of shield and buckler, and stand up for mine help", Psalm35:1- 2.* By this, let every witchcraft judgment, every ordinance and dark throne in the heavenly established against my marriage scatter, in the name of Jesus.

O Lord crush to pieces and grind to powder altars assign against my life. Save me from the hands of the wicked and let every power searching the oracle to scatter my marriage die. Every seed of marital failure in my life die. Any power wickedly interested in my marriage die. Every labour of the enemy against my marriage meet double failure. Enemies of my soul shall not prevail against me. For it is written, *"And they shall fight against thee, but they shall not prevail against thee for I am with thee, saith the Lord, to deliver thee" Jeremiah* **1:19.** Let every ancestral altar working against my life catch fire and roast to ashes. Let every altar crying against me roast to ashes. Let every demonic chain holding me captive break, and let every mad spirit that gathered round me scatter, in the name of Jesus.

Root of bitterness in my life dry up by fire in the name of Jesus. Wicked powers that say my problem is not enough, I dash you my problems, carry it away in the name of Jesus. Every arrow of automatic failure targeted against my life backfire by fire, in the name of Jesus. Every problem that finds its way into my life walk out now by fire. Every diviner working against my life receive total blindness and madness, in the name of Jesus.

O Lord, break to pieces bows of wicked warriors fashioned against me. Thou witchcraft pot caging my star break, thou cage of bewitchment fashioned against my destiny be roasted to ashes. Thou witchcraft rope that tied me down to one spot break and catch fire, in the name of Jesus. Thou generational curse troubling me break. Thou sour water of sorrow and river of darkness flowing into my life, dry up in the name of Jesus.
O Lord, speak woe to curses in my family line. Blood of Jesus break every curse and covenant of failure in my life. Every iron like problem, iron like curses and covenants troubling my life break in the name of Jesus. Every witchcraft battle at the edge of breakthrough be defeated. Every curse of *'no mercy and helpers for you,* in my life break. O Lord, restore my finance hundred fold, as promised in *Joel* 2:25, **"And I will restore to you the years that the locust hath eaten, the cankerworm, and the caterpillar, and the palmerworm, my great army which I sent among you"**

Any power caging my helpers from reaching me die. I shake and destroy every mountain fashioned against me. I reject and nullify evil decrees of marital failure in my life. I nullify evil statement against my life. I nullify wicked action of the enemy against my life, for **"who is he that saith, and it cometh to pass, when the Lord commandeth it not? Lamentation 3:37**. Therefore every action and moves of the enemy against me shall not stand but fail, in the name of Jesus.

Power of delay release your grip upon my life now in the name of Jesus. Any hidden altar of my father's house and of my mother's house speaking failure into my life be roasted to ashes. Any idol of my father's house supervising me for evil die. You power of my father's house holding me in bondage lose your hold now and die. Every harassing power delegated against me fall down and die, in the name of Jesus.

Every open gate of poverty in my life close by fire in the name of Jesus. I break, destroy and walk out from evil cage and spiritual prison hindering me to mountain top. For as it is written, *"Although you have been forsaken and hated, with no one travelling through, I will make you the everlasting pride and the joy of all generations" Isaiah 60:15.* Therefore, my testimony what are you doing in the camp of the enemy arise, come and locate me by fire. By this, I nullify wicked decree and ordinance against me for the Lord is capable of *blotting out the hand writing of ordinances that was against us, which was contrary to us, and took it out of the way, nailing it to his cross" Colossians 2*

CHAPTER SEVEN

PRAYER THAT REVERSES EVIL PRONOUNCEMENT

O Lord break the teeth of eaters of flesh delegated against me. Strike the cheekbone of wicked powers making incantations against me. Let every evil tongue fashioned against me be revoked. Nullify every prophesy that is not of God against me. Let wicked pronouncement and curse of no way to progress, no way to marriage, no way for good job pronounced against me be nullified and be revoked, in the name of Jesus. Let every strange tongue speaking evil against me cease by fire and die. Paralyze and destroy evil tongue using my past to curse my future. For it is written', my God, *"..shall increase my greatness, and comfort me on every side". Psalm 71:21.*

Every negative speech, negative language, negative voice or word spoken against me be nullified. I decree civil war and confusion into the camp of house hold enemies and territorial powers delegated against me. Power of resurrection, heal my spirit, soul and body, so that my family and I may not groan under bondage of oppression, suppression and afflictions in the name of Jesus.

Every evil remark against my marriage be nullified, by blood of Jesus. Every enemy of my soul meet double failure. *"Let my persecutor be put to shame, but keep me from shame, let them be terrified but keep me from terror. Bring on them the day of disaster, destroy them with double destruction" Jeremiah 17:18.* Every prophecy of darkness against my marriage be nullified. Every arrow of confusion fired against my future, back fire by fire. Every roadblock on my way to success be destroyed by fire. Every mountain on my way to success I roll you into the Red Sea.

O Lord save me from arrow of the wicked. *"keep me as the apple of your eyes, hide me in the shadow of your wings" Psalm 17:18.* Thou host of heaven arrest and execute strongman and powers attach to my cause. Arrow of marital stagnancy and failure in my life, release me and go back to your sender. Thou wicked power holding vigil against me run mad and die. Thou evil gate standing against me I pull you down. Thou wall of Jericho and pillar of failure separating me from marital life, scatter into desolation.

Every artillery and bombardment of enemies against my life and destiny backfire by fire, in the name of Jesus. Every arrow of darkness fired against my star backfire by fire. Hence, I fire back arrow of marital failure against me. I fire back every arrow of stagnancy fired against me. Therefore, I command every evil arrow fired against me to go back to the sender and consume them, in the name of Jesus.

(NOW SING THIS SONG· WITH HOLY ANGER IN YOU)
EVIL ARROW GO BACK TO THE SENDER
EVIL ARROW GO BACK TO THE SENDER
EVIL ARROW GO BACK TO THE SENDER
EVIL ARROW GO BACK TO THE SENDER

Where God wants me to be, where God prepared for me, I shall walk into it. My marriage shall not crawl. I shall be unstopable by wicked forces, I shall be
unmolested by wicked powers, I shall be a champion before my detractors in the name of Jesus. Hence every evil bird flying for my sake shall fall down and die. For it is written, ***"Though you soar like the eagle and make your nest among the stars, from there I will bring you down, declares the LORD. Obadiah* 1:4.**

O Lord save my head and that of my spouse *(mention his/her name if you are in courtship)* from evil arrows, wicked enchantments and evil curses, in the name of Jesus. With your rod of iron break and scatter every gang up against me. Fire your arrow of disunity into their midst and scatter their wicked plans against me. Hence, no worker of iniquity shall succeed in my life. Amen.

O Lord, send thunder, fire, hailstone and lightning from heaven into the camps of my enemies. For it is written, **upon the wicked He shall rain snares, fire and brimstone, and an horrible tempest: this shall be the portion of their cup" Psalm 11:6.** Scatter the camp of my enemies and bring their counsel to naught. Let every re-grouping of the enemies against my life scatter. For it is written, **"The strangers shall fade away, and be afraid out of their close places. Psalm 18:45.** By this, enemies .of my soul shall rise no more but fade away, in the name of Jesus. Amen.

BURY MARITAL DISGRACE

O Lord, save and lift me above standard of the enemy. Let peace reign on my wedding day. Plant seed of respect and accord in my marriage. In my day to day activities make me to understand stupidity and repercussions involved in wickedness and madness of folly that sink marriage. My marriage appear, let any power or personality occupying my seat be unseated by fire. Hence, I pull down every witchcraft power and principalities standing as giants against my life.

Thou spirit of coffin fashioned against me swallow your owner. Every trap set by enemies to disgrace me before my wedding day catch your owner. Every satanic net spread for my sake catch your owner. Any power working hard to frustrate my efforts from getting married die. For it is written, **"whoso diggeth a pit shall fall therein and he that** *rolleth a stone, it will return upon him" Proverbs 26:27.* I release myself from spiritual slavery. I nullify and cancel evil treaty signed by me in the dream that places me under satanic oath. Every vision killer assign to divert my attention from fruitful marriage die.

Thou spirit of demotion in my life, today is your burial day, die. Every satanic embargo placed upon my marriage scatter to desolation, in the name of Jesus. Holy Ghost Power, uproot by fire evil tree planted or growing for my sake. Every unprofitable tree trading with my life, trading with my destiny, trading with my joy, trading with my finance, wither and die. Every plantation of wickedness programmed against my destiny, programmed against my marriage, programmed against my joy, programmed against my star, wither to your root and die. Counter supernatural forces of God uproot and destroy every form of pillar standing against my marriage. Thou pillar of witchcraft of my father's house, thou pillar of witchcraft of my mother's house, thou pillar of witchcraft of my In-law's house, thou territorial witchcraft pillar in my environ I pull you down, in the name of Jesus. Every power from the fourth generation of my father's house trying to disgrace me, I pull you down by fire. Family idol and wicked vessels of my parent fashioned against me die. Hence, I command every evil mantle placed

PRAYER FOR SINGLES

upon my marriage to catch fire and roast to ashes, in the name of Jesus. Amen.

Every evil priest hired to inflict calamity and sorrow upon my life run mad with your enchantment and divination. Every instrument of disgrace fashioned against my life backfire by fire in the name of Jesus. Every kingdom of Satan assign against me, be brought down in the name of Jesus. O God of Elijah, with your hammer of fire nail to death any power that doesn't want me to get married. Thou star of my life reject command of the enemy. Thou wicked mountain opposing my star receive divine judgment of destruction. Thou witchcraft pot caging my star, your time is up, therefore break. Every satanic cloud covering the star of my marriage clear off by fire. My star and testimony, what are you doing in the cage of the enemy, arise, receive deliverance and shine, in the name of Jesus. You strongman blocking my star from experiencing testimony fall down and die. Thou star of my life return from every unprofitable journey in the name of Jesus. Thou sun, moon, and star, arise and shine to my glory.

Special announcement: I announce obituary and burial of power of darkness caging my star, emptying my star or destroying my star, in the name of Jesus. *(Now point your finger to the earth and say like this)* Thou earth today is your feast day, open by fire and consume wicked forces fashioned against my destiny.

Therefore, I command marriage killers, vision killers, wicked arrow shooting spirit, wicked pursuers, star hijackers and poverty distributing spirit in my life, to come here right now, gather together and enter this pit. Today is today; the battle line is drawn. I command you to enter the pit and be buried, in the name of Jesus. O earth, swallow the Goliath of my life. For it is written; *"But those who seek my soul to destroy it, shall go into the lower part of the earth. They shall fall by the sword: they shall be a portion for foxes" Psalm 63:9-10.* Strangers of darkness in my life die. Robbers of darkness in my life die.

I shall not sink in the sea of life. For it is written, *"When thou passeth through the waters, I will be with thee: and through the rivers, they shall not overflow thee:*
when thou walkest through the fire, thou shalt not be buried, neither shall the flame kindle upon thee" Isaiah 43:2. Hence, I replace mourning cloth in my life with cloth of joy and grave cloth to be replaced with cloth of life and fruitfulness, in the name of Jesus. Amen.

CHAPTER EIGHT

WARFARE AGAINST MARRIAGE CRUSHERS

O Lord, give me wisdom to see my marriage through, for wisdom is better than weapons of war. Give me skill that brings success, for skill is mightier than force. Let divine blessing swallow quarrel that may arise to scatter my marriage. For ***"the blessing of the LORD it maketh rich, and he addeth no sorrow with it" Proverbs 10:22.*** Therefore, let every power that wants to steal my joy be put to shame in the name of Jesus.

O Lord, quench the lamp of the wicked, for the lamp of the wicked is sin. Dry their fountain, it is poisonous. Paralyze and destroy every move and activity of the enemy against me for, ***"If a snake bites before it is charmed, there is no profit for the charmer" Ecclesiastes 0: 11***. Let wicked powers and personalities behind my marriage meet double failure. Weaken the energy of my enemies, dry the source of their power and strength.

With the support of the living God, I shall build my home. No mock or contrary power shall swallow it or pull it down, in the name of Jesus. Every mocker of my marriage shall be put to shame in the order of Samballat and Tobiah. O Lord place every in-law under check from scattering my marriage. Let every oppressor assign against me harvest wretchedness and failure. Let every ritual targeted against my marriage backfire by fire. I shall not go into the grave childless. Amen.

Power of God; scatter every wicked program fashion against me. Every lion roaring against my marriage die. Every power assign to rob my marriage die. Fortified gathering of enemies against me, scatter like packs of cards, become desolate like abandon settlement. Thou power in charge of my situation, in the-day and at night you shall be uncomfortable. No matter how big your bed is, it shall be too hot and too short for you to stretch out. Your blanket shall be tattered and too narrow to wrap round you. Thou satanic informant assign to monitor me become deaf and dumb, in the name of Jesus. O Lord, render my enemies powerless over my situations and let every voice of unfriendly friend around me become useless. As from today, unfriendly friends around me shall scatter, in the name of Jesus. Blood of Jesus repair damage done to my life through unfriendly friend. By this Lord, place them in perpetual quietness, perpetual soberness and total confusion.
Owner of evil load, carry your load, my life is not your candidate. I refuse to be victim of marriage. I recover my virtues hundred fold from the hand of the enemy. Wicked strategy designed to scatter my marriage be frustrated. Solutions to my situation

appear now and take over my life in Jesus name. Amen.

CHAPTER NINE

WARFARE AGAINST SPIRIT SPOUSE

(This topic is a must for people harassed in the dream through sex or, threatened by strange men or strange women. They should pray this with fire and with,
aggression in them)

O Lord turn me to giant before spirit spouse, protect me with power of "touch not". Build for me a home of peace and joy for the *"builder of a house has greater honour"* Hebrew 3:3. My marriage shall not be taken over by strange men or strange women in the name of Jesus. Any contrary power assign to take over my position, receive total destruction and shame in the name of Jesus. Hence, I reject and renounce every association with spirit spouse wife, in the name of Jesus.

Every evil jewelry, brooches, earrings, and ornaments in my possession that is working against me catch fire in the name of Jesus. Satanic ring from the
ocean, satanic ring from the second heaven, satanic ring from wicked powers aimed to disgrace me or destabilize my marriage catch fire in the name of Jesus. Spiritual wedding materials in my possession catch fire and burn to ashes. My marriage certificate in the spirit I reject you, burn

to ashes in the name of Jesus. My spirit wedding ring, I pull you off and reject you, burn to ashes in the name of Jesus. My spirit wedding gown/suit and wedding shoes I pull you off, I reject you, therefore burn to ashes, in the name of Jesus.

Thou spirit children attached to this marriage die in the name of Jesus. Best man and Best lady involved in the spirit wedding die and rise no more, in the name of Jesus. Wicked spirit priest and organizers involved in the spirit wedding die, in the name of Jesus. Thou wicked power assign against me the table has turn against you therefore run mad and die. My effort to build a prosperous and God fearing home shall not be ruin by you, in the name of Jesus.

Holy Ghost Fire, burn to ashes organs of wicked powers making love with me in the dream. Thou spirit children involved in this wedding as a result of previous love die. Evil strangers in my life die. Hence, I bind and destroy every contrary controlling forces and power of marital failure in my life.

My marriage to spirit spouse be dissolved, in the name of Jesus. Every wicked judgment passed against me as I divorce my spirit spouse be nullified, illegal and of no effect in the name of Jesus. I gain my liberty through the power in the blood of Jesus that covers me and by the power of the Holy Ghost that is with me. Hence, I release myself from spirit marriage and children in the name of Jesus.

I paralyze power of evil manipulation against my life. My enemies fall into deep sleep and rise no more. God of Elijah, descend your fierce fire from heaven, consume monster of the sea fashioned against me. Every violent and destructive storm that rises against me from the grave be silent, for there is no connection between the living and the dead. Every stubborn marine power assign to disrupt my marriage die. Marine witchcraft causing weariness in my life, fall down and die, in the name of Jesus.

Rescue me O Lord from enemies and foes that are too strong for me. Host of heaven turn the dwelling place of wicked powers against me into dissolation in the order of Sodom and Gomorrah. Every organized witchcraft power that vow I shall remain single for life scatter by fire. All friends of darkness in my life robbing me of my joy be exposed and be disgraced. Family spirit spouse troubling my life be exposed and be disgraced. O Lord let every demon of adversity, demon of miscarriage, demon of untimely death, demon of affliction, demon of poverty assigned to destroy my joy and destiny die. Let every deposit and property of spirit spouse in my possession die and roast to ashes, in the name of Jesus.

Every impersonating power in my dream die. Every forest that approved my spirit marriage be consumed by fire. Every rock of darkness that approved my spirit marriage be blasted by thunder fire of God. Every ocean, sea or water that that approved my spirit marriage dry up by fire.

Thou strange power that wants to disgrace me to square one of life, that wants me to crawl instead of walking, that wants me to turn back instead of moving forward in life die, in the name of Jesus. I shall not build for others to take over or plant for others to harvest the fruits of my labour, in the name of Jesus. No power either near or far away from me shall stand against my marital breakthrough. For it is written, *"No weapon that is formed against thee shall prosper, and every tongue that shall rise against thee in judgment thou shall condemn. This is the heritage of the servants of the LORD" Isaiah 54:17* Amen. By this, my marriage shall not experience spiritual or physical reverse, spiritual or physical backwardness, spiritual or physical delay, spiritual or physical deadlock, in the name of Jesus. Amen

CHAPTER TEN

PRAYER FOR RIGHT SPOUSE

O Lord fill my heart with *"joy and gladness instead of grief, a song of praise instead of sorrow" Isaiah 61:3.* Give me understanding and discipline partner, full of prudence, wisdom and knowledge. Save me from marrying a bitter-hearted partner, a partner who is a snare, whose heart is a trap and whose hands are chains of captivity. Therefore my spouse, *"wisdom will save you from the ways of wicked men, from men whose words are perverse" Proverbs 2:12.*

O Lord let my marriage hold now so that I might *be like a tree-planted by the rivers of water, that bringeth forth his fruit in his seasons, his leaf also shall not wither, and whatsoever he doeth shall prosper "Psalm* 1:3. Hence I shall find the bone of my bone and the flesh of my flesh in the name of Jesus. As father Abraham married Sarah and starts new lineage so will I find my spouse. As Isaac married Rebecca and brought forth seedlings so shall my marriage witness fruitfulness. As Jacob succeeded in having the twelve tribes of Israel so shall my children be candidate of greatness. As Moses married in foreign land and made divine history so shall my marriage fulfill historical achievement and testimonies, in the name of Jesus.

CHAPTER ELEVEN

PRAYER FOR MALE ONLY
THIS SESSION IS MEANT FOR MALES ONLY

O Lord, empower me to locate the bone of my bone and the flesh of my flesh. Don't allow this year pass me by without having my right choice in marriage. For you said concerning me in **_Psalm 2: 7_**. **_"You are my son, today I have become your Father. Ask of me, and I will make the nations your inheritance the end of the earth your possession"_** By this I pull off and tear to pieces garment of bachelor in my life. I disassociate my life from bachelorhood, from speech of bachelorhood and attitude of bachelorhood, in the name of Jesus. Every power in my foundation saying I shall not wed be exposed and be defeated. Divine sword of God, bring silence upon every power waging war against me. My fountain receive divine blessing for it is written, **_"May your fountain be blessed and may you rejoice in the Wife of your youth" Proverbs 5:18._** For **_"...blessed is the man who trusts in the Lord" Jeremiah 17:7_**

As father Abraham married Sarah and left his father's house to form his lineage so will I form my lineage, in the name of Jesus. By this Lord, make my wife a rare jewel within and around me.

For it is written *"He who finds a wife finds what is good and receives favour from the LORD"* **Proverbs 18:22.** My wife, where are you? Appear by fire for the fulfillment of our marriage. I am ready, my soul and body is ready for marriage.

Hence I command every local Jericho wall separating me from my wife, to be pulled down by fire. I paralyze and destroy every tact of satanic spinster sent from the pit of hell to destroy me in the order of Samson before Delilah. Thou Delilah delegated against me, my laps is not your candidate therefore fall down and die. Thou dark woman of Babylon delegated against me I kill you, I kill your strange children, I dissolve any marriage between me and you in the name of Jesus.

Every Pharaoh pursuing my Moses, enter the Red Sea and die. Hence I speak woe against vessel of stagnancy delegated against me. I speak destruction against
wicked root and powers assigned against me. I speak paralysis unto wicked plantations standing against my joy. At the end I shall marry my right spouse and laugh and laugh and laugh, in the name of Jesus. Amen.

CHAPTER TWELVE

PRAYER FOR FEMALES ONLY

THE SESSION IS MEANT FOR FEMALE ONLY

Lord Jesus, display your vast wealth of love, splendor and glory upon me. Surprise the least to the greatest in my family concerning my marital situation. Whenever my husband sees me Lord, let me have lovely look before him like a royal princess, an inestimable Jewel. At the end of it all support me to move to my husband's house in full scale laughter and joy in the name of Jesus. Hence, I shall arise and step into my rightful marital home. Amen.

O Lord with your power empower me to locate the bone of my bone and the flesh of my flesh. Thou right man of my destiny locate me by fire for where my husband stays there I shall stay. His people shall be my people and his God(Lord Jesus) shall be my God.

O Lord, fight for me, be furious in your anger against wicked powers that vowed I shall be single and unmarried. Dress me with divine colourful garment that will make me irresistible before my beloved ones. Thou garment of spinsterhood on me your time has expire therefore I pull you off. Let wise men and women of my husband support me by fire. I shall not be kicked out nor shall my goods be thrown out of my husband's house, in the name of Jesus. By this no power or personality shall engineer divorce in my marriage in the name of Jesus. Divorce shall not find place in my marriage neither shall my marriage experience affliction or misfortune. No girl or woman shall replace me in my matrimonial home in the name of Jesus. As mother Sarah left her father's house and wedded father Abraham so shall I leave my father's house and be wedded to my husband, in the name of Jesus.

Fire Sword of God bring divine silence upon every power waging war against me. Every power in my foundation that refuse to let me go die, Every local Jericho blocking my husband from locating me I pull you down. I speak woe against evil vessel dedicated to bring my life to stagnancy. I speak destruction unto every wicked root holding me captive. Therefore, thou wicked roots and branches troubling my life wither and die, in the name of Jesus.

CHAPTER THIRTEEN

WEDDING DAY PRAYER

(Apart from your usual prayer before the wedding day, make sure you pray this prayer with violence a day or two before wedding. Don't allow Satan to cheat you.)

My wedding day appear by fire and be sealed with approval in heaven. My marriage, come to pass now for I am waiting. My thirst and hunger for marriage shall be crowned with testimonies. My wedding day shall be a day of peace, a day of joy, a day of blessing and a day of success. O Lard my God, pour blessings upon me. On my wedding day I shall not encounter death nor shall my family or visitors encounter such, in the name of Jesus. ***Deliver my life from the sword, my precious life from the power of the dogs" Psalm 22:20***. On my wedding day, death shall pass over me, sickness and diseases shall pass over me, tragedy shall pass over me, poverty shall pass over me, wicked arrows shall pass over, in the name of Jesus.

O Lord disgrace every testimony and miracle arrester assign to pull me down. Your commandment that a man shall leave his father's house and join his spouse shall be fulfilled in my life. Therefore, I command my day of Cana of Galilee to appear now, for my wedding day is not negotiable. Every satanic plan aimed at disrupting my marriage shall scatter, in the name of Jesus. Thou satanic prophesy pronounced against me your time has expired therefore meet failure. Songs of joy and happiness fill my soul and body. I shall not harvest death, sorrow, poverty or failure but joy, fruitfulness, blessings, progress and breakthroughs, in the name of Jesus. Amen

Lord Jesus write my wedding invitation cards yourself. Capture right minds that shall attend my wedding. Let my visitors turn up as one man. Let praises and thanksgiving be the order of the day. Arrest the minds of people that shall serve food on that day from colluding with wicked ones to perpetrate evil. By this, foods served shall not kill, drinks taken shall not turn be poisonous, and seats offered shall not be death traps, in the name of Jesus. **"Let me not be put to shame, O Lord for I have cried out to you" Psalm 31:17**. O Lord, touch the heart of my family in support of my wedding. Blood of Jesus paralyze and destroy any gift or gifts incubated with evil powers. Expose and disgrace any person or group of persons with evil intention against me. Let free offer, valuable gifts and support come from the known and unknown. Let me receive unpolluted precious gifts in the order of the Israelites before the Egyptians on the day of pass over in Egypt. Therefore render every strange gift assign for my sake powerless and useless.

Every stumbling block assign to hurt my marriage be consumed by fire. *"May all who gloat over my distress be put to shame and confusion, may all who exalt themselves over me be clothed with shame and disgrace" Psalm* **36:26**. Hence Lord, render useless and powerless any witch or wizard that may attend my wedding. Blood of Jesus dissolve and destroy evil sacrifice carried out or about to be carried out against me. I command evil hands that may be stretched against me or placed upon me to wither. Hence, let every croocketh path before me become straight. Let every mountain before me be leveled and every valley in my life be filled, in the name of Jesus.

I render useless every charm targeted against me. Every arrow prepared against me backfire by fire. Every negative prayer targeted against me be nullified. Every marital defeat fashioned against me be defeated by fire, in the name of Jesus. Prosperity in this year, success in this year, breakthrough in this year, locate me by fire. In my journey to marital altar, enemies shall not triumph over me, in the name of Jesus. My wedding program shall not be supplanted by programs of darkness. Every contrary program targeted against me shall not stand but fail in the name of Jesus. Therefore, I say woe!, woe!!, woe!!! against evil program targeted against me. By the same power that separate night from day, separate me from power of loneliness. O Lord my God, turn my sorrow to joy, turn my loneliness to fruitfulness. For it is written, *"He turned the desert unto pools of water and the parched ground into flowing springs, there lie brought the hungry to live, and they founded a city where they could settle" Psalm 107:35-36.* By this, let east wind blow away incantations and enchantments spoken against me. Let every contrary wind against me become favourable.

Holy Ghost Power, charge my wedding zone and home with fire. Confuse and scatter wicked logistic assign by enemies to disgrace and disorganize my marriage. O Lord you are God of wonders, perform wonders in my life. Holy Spirit padlock the mouth of hostile friends and neighbors fashioned against me and let there be division of tongue in their evil camps. For, *"As the mountains surround Jerusalem, so the Lord surrounds his people both now and for ever more" Amen. Psalm 125:2.*

O Lord let my spouse trust in the Lord and not in his/ her personal understanding. My spouse, you shall experience good health, your bones shall experience nourishment. Sound judgment shall come forth from you. *"when you walk, your steps will not be hampered, when you run, you will not stumble" Proverbs 4:12.* By this any strongman or woman assign to supervise your life shall stumble and die, in the name of Jesus.

O Lord perfect my marriage because you are a perfect God. For it is written, ***"The Lord will perfect that which concerneth me" Psalm* 138:8.** Therefore, my marriage be precious than gold and be sweeter than honey. Let knowledge, wisdom and understanding take over my marital home during and after my wedding. Blessings and favour of God make my life your habitation. My marriage shall not experience frustration or experience affliction, tragedy or failure, in the name of Jesus. As from now on, I claim uncommon success, uncommon increase and fruitfulness, in the name of Jesus. Amen

CHAPTER FOURTEEN

MY FAVOUR AND MERCY IS TODAY

Holy Ghost, program my destiny to uncommon success and increase. Thou wicked power assign to pull me off my marital path of breakthrough you shall not locate me. My stars come out of your hidden place. Arise and shine before men and women for the Lord has broken wicked yoke surrounding you. As it is written, **"For now will I break his yoke from off thee and will burst thy bonds in sunder" Nahum 1:13.** By this, no man or woman shall write me off, in the name of Jesus Amen.

"If clouds are full of water, they pour rain upon the earth" Eccl. 11:3, rain that falls after much expectations bring joy to heart. Therefore Lord, let your
unpolluted and divine favour pour upon me. Let your favour incubate my life, let your favour incubate my destiny. Let it incubate my steps, incubate my future and understanding now. Let zeal to pray envelope my house so that it shall be **"a house of prayer to all nations" Isaiah 56: 7.**

Oh God arise and envelope me with divine favour. Let your favour manifest in my life by fire today. Favour of God envelope my star; envelope my destiny for signs and wonders. Thou songs of joy in my mouth you shall not grow faint. Merited and unmerited favour of God and of men locate me by fire. As daylight brings brightness, and stars of the sky bring joy to heart, the door that leads to my marriage shall open and bring me joy in the name of Jesus. Amen.

(NOW BE ON YOUR KNEE AND PRAY)
O Lord, change my marital anthem for good. Change it from, who shall make me warm in my closet? Who shall hug me as spouse? Who shall I discuss my children with? Who shall console me in time of needs? Who shall laugh genuine laughter with me in time of laughter to better situation of my liking.

Therefore Lord, change my song to: "This is my only one, my dear one who I love most in life. The apple of my eyes and flower in my garden. Fake kisses are gone. I have found my genuine one". O God fill my mouth with songs of Solomon. I am in need of a spouse. Do it now Lord and thank you for answering my prayer. Amen. (NOW STAND UP)

CHAPTER FIFTEEN

STRONG POSITIVE CONFESSIONS

In this prayer Lord, may *the words of my mouth and the meditation of my heart be pleasing in your sight".' Psalm* 19: 14. My tongue receive fire and power, speak goodness to my life. My mouth be filled with praises and honour unto God. My heart be filled with joy and gladness. Thou Goliath in my life die for my marriage is not negotiable. I shall marry in the land of the living and experience no evil carry over after my wedding Amen.

My season and time of marriage appear, come to fulfillment. My destiny, arise and shine. All time and season shall work to my favour, in the name of Jesus. Every disappointment and sorrow I pass through, weeks back, months back and years back shall turn to joy and blessing, in the name of Jesus. I shall not miss divine timing in my marriage. As I sow unto my marriage, so will I harvest multiple joy and success, in the name of Jesus. **"Listen to my cry for help, my King and my God, for to you I pray" Psalm 3:7.** O God my father, perfect your miracle in my life.

Divine salt of God that bring changes to life appear in my life today. Thou eagle of my life, you must fly high, therefore fly and occupy your position now. My heart rejoice for sorrow is not your portion. Today the LORD shall perfect my marriage, cleanse my garment of shame and build my marriage on solid rock of breakthrough.

For the Bible says, **"He is the Rock, his works are perfect, and all his ways are just A faithful God Who does no wrong, upright and just is He" Deuteronomy 32:4.** During and after my wedding my Lord shall favour me. Testimonies shall fill my mouth. I shall excel in my undertakings. Calamity shall not locate me neither shall bad news filter into my ears. Coupon paper shall not replace my marriage certificate in the physical or in the spirit. My marriage shall be nourished with honey out of the rock. The olive in my hand shall not dry or wither, in the name of Jesus.

I claim life not death, prosperity not destruction, in the name of Jesus. Dreadful disease of Egypt shall not be my portion. Afflictions in my life shall die and rise no more. Every childless sword fashioned against me shall not prosper. Powers that steal joy and gladness shall not locate me. At the end, I shall not sing songs of lamentation or songs of sorrow, in the name of Jesus.

O Lord enable me to walk in your ways, and to keep your commands and decrees so that I might be a blessing to this generation. For it is written,**"It shall come to pass, that before they call, I will answer; and while they are yet speaking I will** *hear" Isaiah 65:24.* Hence, I declare as follows upon my life:- My purse and bank account shall not go bankrupt or drained by powers of darkness. My assets shall not be swallowed by liabilities nor my profits swallowed by losses, in the name of Jesus. My clothes and sandals shall not wear out by forces of poverty and lack. My expectations shall come to pass while my enemies shall bow, in the name of Jesus. Amen.' '

I pronounce failure and defeat against powers and forces of the night. Any giant waiting to harvest my breakthrough shall summersault and die. No giant or power
of darkness shall be strong enough to destroy my marriage. No plague or disaster, no lingering or illness, shall' take over my home, in the name of Jesus. No trial or temptation shall travail over my marriage. No power of my father's house, or power of my mother's house, or power of my in-law's house or territorial power fashion against me shall succeed in the name of Jesus. *"I am against you, o destroying mountain, you who destroy the whole earth" Jeremiah 51:25.*

SPECIAL ANNOUNCEMENT: - Satan, the host of heaven issue royal decree in my support, saying, "receive liberty, marry and be fruitful by fire" Hence, I decree uncommon success, uncommon increase, uncommon opportunities, favour and breakthrough into my life and destiny in the name of Jesus.

I receive baptism of wisdom to end all struggles. Miracles, signs and wonders shall envelope my life. In the morning it shall be well with me, at noon it shall be well with me, in the evening and at night it shall be well with me in the name of Jesus. My marriage shall not experience spiritual enslavement, physical or material enslavement, in the name of Jesus. Amen.

DIVINE'CLOSURE:- I close every door I open to Satan. I close every door that gives Satan opportunity to steal from me. I close every door that lead to sin, that lead to fornication, that lead to poverty, tragedy, sorrow and loneliness, in the name of Jesus.

NOW OPEN:- I open doors that lead to marital breakthrough, that lead to prosperity, joy, progress, uncommon success and favour of God, in the name of Jesus. As these doors open, no power of darkness shall close against me in the name of Jesus, Amen. I command all problems causing secret tears in my life to receive divine solution by fire. My night of troubles are over, my nightmares have ended in the name of Jesus. I say bye to sources, fountains and mountains of marital impossibilities in my life as *"All my enemies will*

be ashamed and dismayed, they will turn back in sudden disgrace" **Amen Psalm 6:10**

OPERATION BACK TO SENDER
As a result of my prayer today, I fire back every, arrow of discomfort and failure that may be fired at me by enemies. I therefore return arrow for arrow, fire for fire, bullets for bullets, tongues for tongues, action for action, pursuits for pursuits, in the name of Jesus. I roll Rock of Ages against any power that may attack me. My enemies shall bow, fall and rise no more in the name of Jesus Amen.

PRAYER FOR SINGLES

FINAL THANKSGIVING

1 sought the LORD, and he answered me, he delivered me from all my fears" Psalm 34:4. For this, I thank you Lord for turning my disappointments to appointments and for burning my case file before you into ashes. I thank you Lord because you re-adjust me, re-position me and re-locate me for a wonderful marital breakthrough. I thank you Lord that my victory shall be permanent, in Jesus name, Amen.

NOW SING THIS SONG AS SIGN OF CONFIRMATION
IT SHALL BE PERMANENT
IT SHALL BE PERMANENT
WHAT THE LORD HAS DONE FOR ME
IT SHALL BE PERMANENT. AMEN
Sing it again

SEAL YOUR PRAYER.

Lord JESUS, I seal my prayer with your blood and incubate it with fire of protection. Thou angels in heaven announce and seal my prayer.
At the end of this prayer, I shall give testimony to works of God in my life. Testimony swallower shall not swallow my testimony in the name of Jesus. By this, no wicked hands, legs, mouth or power shall unseal my testimonies.

SHARE THE GRACE

May the grace of our Lord Jesus Christ, the love of God and the sweet fellowship of the Holy Spirit be with me now and forever more Amen. Surely His goodness and mercy shall follow me and abide in me forever and ever. Amen.

YOU HAVE BATTLES TO WIN

TRY THESE BOOKS

1. COMMAND THE DAY

Each day of the week is loaded with meanings and divine assurance. God did not create each day of the week for the fun of it. Blessings, success, gifts, resources, hopes, portfolios, duties, rights, prophecies, warnings and challenges, are loaded in each day.

Do you know the language, command or decree you can use to claim what belongs to you in each day of the week? Do you know in Christendom, Monday can be equated to one of the days of creation in Genesis chapter one? Do you know creation lasted for six days and God rested on the seventh day? What day of the week can Christian equate as the first day of the week, if we follow Christian calendar? What day can we call day seven?

This book shall give insight to these questions. It shall explain how you can command each day of the week according to creation in the book of Genesis chapter one.

Above all, you shall exercise your right and claim what is hidden in each day of the week.

Check for this in *COMMAND THE DAY*

PRAYER TO REMEMBER DREAMS

A lot of people are passing through this spiritual epidemic on a daily basis. Their dream life is epileptic, having no ability to remember all dreams they dream, or sometimes forget everything entirely. This is nothing but spiritual havoc you need to erase from your spiritual record.

The answer to every form of spiritual blackout caused by spiritual erasers is found in, *PRAYER TO REMEMBER DREAMS.*

100% CONFESSSIONS AND PROPHECIES TO LOCATE HELPERS

This is a wonderful book on confessions and prophecies to locate helpers and helpers to locate you. It is a prayer book loaded with over two thousand (2,000) prayer points.

The book unravels how to locate unknown helpers, prayers to arrest mind of helpers and prayers for manifestation after encounter with helpers.

ANOINTING FOR ELEVENTH HOUR HELP

This book tells much of what to do at injury hour called eleventh hour. When you read and use this book as prescribed fear shall vanish in your life when pursuing a project, career or contract.

PRAYER TO LOCATE HELPERS

Our divine helper is God. He created us to be together and be of help to one another. In the midst of no help we lost out, ending our journey in the wilderness.

There are keys assign to open right doors of life. You need right key to locate your helpers. Enough is enough; of suffering in silence.

With this book, you shall locate your helpers while your helpers shall locate you

FIRE FOR FIRE PRAYER BOOK

This prayer book is fast at answering spiritual problems. It is a bulldozer prayer book, full of prayers all through. It is highly recommended for night vigil. Testimonies are pouring in daily from users of this book across the world!

PRAYER FOR THE FRUIT OF THE WOMB

This prayer book is children magnet. By faith and believe in God Almighty, as soon as you use this book open doors to child bearing shall be yours. Amen

PRAYER FOR PREGNANT WOMEN

This is a spiritual prayer book loaded with prayers of solution for pregnant women. As soon as you take in, the prayers you shall pray from day one of conception to the day of delivery are written in this book.

WARFARE IN THE OFFICE

It is high time you pray prayers of power must change hands in office. Use this book and liberate yourself from every form of office yoke.

MY MARRIAGE SHALL NOT BREAK

Marriage is corner piece of life, happiness and joy. You need to hold it tight and guide it from wicked intruders and destroyer of homes.

VICTORY OVER SATANIC HOUSE PARTS 1 & 2

Are you a tenant, Land lord bombarded left and right, front and back by wicked people around you?

With this book you shall be liberated from the hooks of the enemy.

DICTIONARY OF DREAMS

This is a must book for every home. It gives accurate details to about **10,000 (Ten thousand) dreams and interpretations,** written in alphabetical order for quick reference and easy digestion. The book portrays spiritual revelations with sound prophetic guidelines. It is loaded with Biblical references and violent prayers.

Ask for yours today.

For Further Enquiries Contact
**THE AUTHOR
EVANGELIST TELLA OLAYERI
P.O. Box 1872 Shomolu Lagos.
Tel: 08023583168**

FROM AUTHOR'S DESK

Authors write for others to digest, gain and broaden intellects. Your comment is therefore needed to arouse others into Christ's bosom.

I therefore implore you to comment on this on this book.

God bless.

Thanks.

Made in the USA
Las Vegas, NV
28 June 2023

73999172R00046